Flowers

by Gail Saunders-Smith

Photo: Bleeding-Heart

Content Consultant:
Deborah Brown, Horticulturist
University of Minnesota Extension Service

Pebble Books
an imprint of Capstone Press

1

Pebble Books

Pebble Books are published by Capstone Press
818 North Willow Street, Mankato, Minnesota 56001
http://www.capstone-press.com

Library of Congress Cataloging-in-Publication Data
Saunders-Smith, Gail.
    Flowers/Gail Saunders-Smith.
        p. cm.
    Includes bibliographical references (p. 23) and index.
    Summary: Simple text and photographs depict the parts of flowers and their pollination.
    ISBN 1-56065-769-3
    1. Flowers—Juvenile literature. 2. Flowers—Fertilizers—Juvenile literature. [1. Flowers.] I. Title
    QK653.S28 1998
    575.6—dc21   98-5049
                                                                          CIP
                                                                           AC

Note to Parents and Teachers

This book describes and illustrates the parts of flowers and how flowers grow. The close picture-text matches support early readers in understanding the text. The text offers subtle challenges with compound and complex sentence structures. This book also introduces early readers to expository and content-specific vocabulary. The expository vocabulary is defined in the Words to Know section. Early readers may need assistance in reading some of these words. Readers also may need assistance in using the Table of Contents, Words to Know, Read More, Internet Sites and Index/Word List sections of the book.

2

Table of Contents

Pistil

Stamens

Petals

Sepals

4

The flower is the part of the plant that makes seeds. A flower has four parts. They are the sepals, petals, stamens, and pistil.

Sepals

Sepals look like leaves. Sepals usually are green. But they can be other colors, too. Sepals cover the flower bud before it opens. They fold back as the flower opens.

Petals

Petals are colored flaps. They are under the sepals when the bud is closed. They open up when a flower blooms. Petals keep the parts inside the flower safe. Their color draws insects.

Some flowers have pockets at the bottom of their petals. These pockets hold nectar. Nectar is a sweet liquid. Some birds, butterflies, and ants drink nectar.

Pollen

Stamens

12

The stamens grow in a circle inside a flower blossom. The tops of the stamens hold pollen. Pollen looks like tiny pieces of sand or powder.

Photo: Center of a Tulip

14

Most pollen is yellow. Pollen can be sticky or dry. Pollen fertilizes flowers. A flower makes seeds if it is fertilized.

Stigma

Pistil

Pollen needs to fall onto the pistil to fertilize a flower. The pistil looks like a small stem. The top of the pistil is the stigma. The stigma is sticky. Pollen sticks to the stigma and enters the pistil. The pistil holds tiny eggs inside. The eggs turn into seeds if they are fertilized.

18

A flower can fertilize itself. Its pollen needs to fall from its stamens onto its pistil. A flower can also fertilize another flower of the same kind. This happens if pollen spreads from flower to flower.

Bees, butterflies, and flies carry pollen from flower to flower. The wind also carries pollen. Pollen helps flowers make seeds.

Photo: Purple Coneflower

Words to Know

bloom—to open up into a flower

fertilize—to start to grow a seed that will make a new plant; a flower is fertilized when pollen joins with eggs inside the pistil; the eggs grow into seeds

liquid—something wet, like water

nectar—a sweet liquid inside a flower that butterflies, ants, and some birds drink

petal—one of the colored flaps or outer parts of a flower

pistil—a stem in the center of the flower; the pistil holds tiny eggs

pollen—tiny pieces on top of stamens in a flower; pollen looks like sand or powder and usually is yellow; pollen joins with the eggs of a flower to make seeds

sepal—the part of the flower that covers the bud before it blooms; sepals look like small leaves

stamen—one of many stems inside a flower blossom; stamens usually are in a circle; the top of a stamen holds pollen

stigma—the top of the pistil; the stigma is sticky to catch pollen

Read More

Barlowe, Dot. *Learning about Flowers.* Mineola, N.Y.: Dover Publications, Inc., 1997.

Bryant-Mole, Karen. *Flowers.* Austin, Tex.: Raintree Steck-Vaughn, 1996.

Butler, Daphne. *What Happens when Flowers Grow.* Austin, Tex.: Raintree Steck-Vaughn, 1995.

Internet Sites

CNPS KIDS PAGE #1
http://www.calpoly.edu/~dchippin/kids1.html

4-H Children's Garden
http://commtechlab.msu.edu/sites/garden/index.html

Kid's Valley Webgarden
http://www.arnprior.com/kidsgarden/index.htm

Index/Word List

ants, 11
bees, 21
birds, 11
bloom, 9
blossom, 13
bud, 7, 9
butterflies, 11, 21
color, 7, 9
eggs, 17
fertilize, 15, 17, 19

flies, 21
flower, 5, 7, 9, 11,
  13, 15, 17, 19, 21
insects, 9
leaves, 7
liquid, 11
nectar, 11
petals, 5, 9, 11
pistil, 5, 17, 19
plant, 5

pockets, 11
pollen, 13, 15, 17,
  19, 21
seeds, 5, 15, 17, 21
sepals, 5, 7, 9
stamens, 5, 13, 19
stem, 17
stigma, 17
wind, 21

Word Count: **270**
Early-Intervention Level: **13**

Editorial Credits
Lois Wallentine, editor; James Franklin, design; Michelle L. Norstad, photo research

Photo Credits
Dembinsky Photo Associates/Anthony Mercieca, 10; Adam Jones, 12; Skip Moody, 20
Images International/Bud Nielson, cover
Chuck Place, 4, 14, 16
Root Resources/Louise K. Broman, 8
Kay Shaw, 6
Richard Hamilton Smith, 1
Michael Worthy, 18